OXFORD

WILD READS

Frogs and Toads

Judy Allen

OXFORD
UNIVERSITY PRESS

This book belongs to:

OXFORD
UNIVERSITY PRESS

Great Clarendon Street, Oxford OX2 6DP

Oxford University Press is a department of the University of Oxford.
It furthers the University's objective of excellence in research, scholarship,
and education by publishing worldwide in

Oxford New York

Auckland Cape Town Dar es Salaam Hong Kong Karachi
Kuala Lumpur Madrid Melbourne Mexico City Nairobi
New Delhi Shanghai Taipei Toronto

With offices in

Argentina Austria Brazil Chile Czech Republic France Greece
Guatemala Hungary Italy Japan Poland Portugal Singapore
South Korea Switzerland Thailand Turkey Ukraine Vietnam

Oxford is a registered trade mark of Oxford University Press
in the UK and in certain other countries

Text © Judy Allen
Illustrations © Steve Roberts
The moral rights of the author have been asserted

Database right Oxford University Press (maker)

This edition 2009

British Library Cataloguing in Publication Data

Data available

ISBN: 978-0-19-911929-5

1 3 5 7 9 10 8 6 4 2

Printed in China
Paper used in the production of this book is a natural,
recyclable product made from wood grown in sustainable forests.
The manufacturing process conforms to the environmental
regulations of the country of origin.

Contents

Where are the frogs and toads?

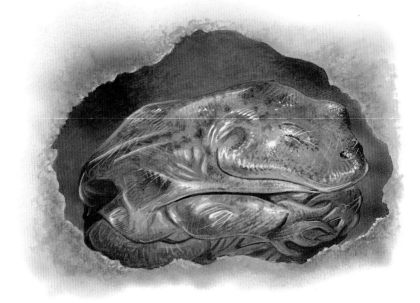

water-holding frog

At this moment, in a desert in Australia, a frog sleeps. It is deep in a burrow under the sand. It is curled up with its eyes closed. It is waiting for the rains to fall.

flying frog

In a jungle in Malaya, a frog flies.
It spreads out its webbed feet and
glides like a bird.
On a lake in India, a frog runs.
It runs fast on top of the water.

midwife toad (Europe)

There are more than 4,000 kinds of frogs and toads.

They live everywhere in the world except the Arctic and the Antarctic where it is too cold.

There have been frogs and toads on the earth for a very long time.

glass frog
(East Africa)

How long is a very long time? 140 million years – or perhaps even longer.

Frogs and toads shared the earth with the dinosaurs.

marsupial frog
(South America)

What are amphibians?

When the world began, the fishes and other animals lived in the oceans.

After a few million years, some animals began to climb out of the water. They learnt to breathe air. They learnt to live on land *and* in water. These animals are called amphibians.

Today, fishes live in water. So do squids and lobsters and eels and whales …

Today, animals live on land. So do birds and insects and spiders and people …

And amphibians live in water *and* on land.

frog

toad

Frogs and toads are amphibians. They can live in ponds and marshes and ditches. And they can live in gardens and fields and woods.

Frogs and toads are very like each other. It isn't easy to know which is which. A good way to tell the difference is to look at the skin.

Most frog skins are smooth and damp.

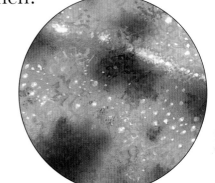

frog skin

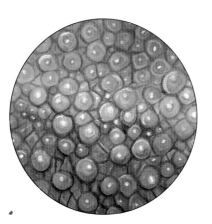

toad skin

Most toad skins have bumps and lumps, called warts. Toad skins are not so damp.

Did you know...
Touching toads can make your hands itchy and sore? **So be careful!**

Can frogs and toads sing?

Frogs and toads have ears and can hear.

Frogs and toads have voices. They can call and sing. Some croak or say, "ribbit, ribbit". Some groan or giggle, some wail or whistle.

bullfrog

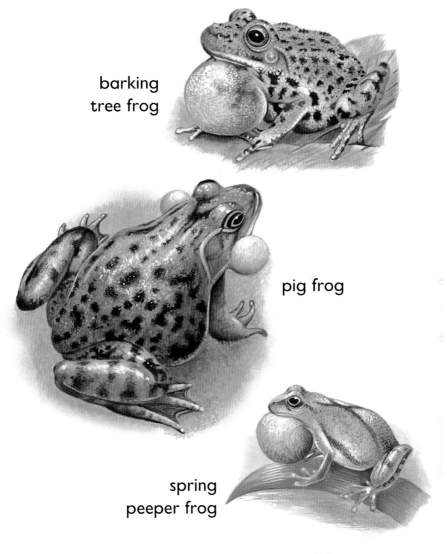

barking
tree frog

pig frog

spring
peeper frog

Some bleat like sheep, grunt like
pigs or bark like dogs. Bullfrogs
bellow, leopard frogs snore, and the
spring peeper frog sounds like
a bird singing.

11

red-eyed tree frog

Frogs and toads sing to call each other, sometimes from a long way away. So they need loud voices.

voice sac of the red-eyed tree frog

A frog can puff out its throat, like a balloon. The balloon is called a voice sac. The voice sac makes the voice louder, much louder.

Some frogs sing alone.
Some frogs sing in groups.

Once, the dinosaurs heard the
frogs singing. Now, if we are lucky,
we can hear the same songs.

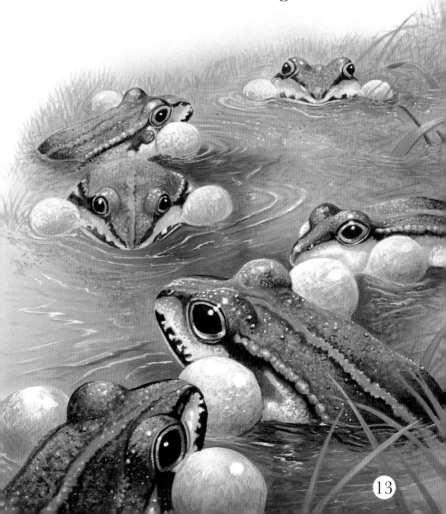

▶ Feet and fingers

Frogs and
toads have
strong back legs.
These help them
to swim, hop and leap.

Frogs and toads
have four fingers
and five toes.

fingers and toes
of a frog

Some tree frogs have
sticky pads on their toes.
This makes it easy for
them to climb.

Some frogs have webbed feet. This means they have skin between their fingers and toes.

Webbed feet help flying frogs to fly.

Webbed feet help swimming frogs to swim.

common frog

▶ Eyes and tongues

southern leopard frog

Frogs and toads have large eyes.
Their eyes bulge and are on top
of their heads, so they can hide
in a pond. Only their eyes and
nose show above the water.

16

Frogs and toads have long tongues. Their tongues are sticky. A frog can unroll its tongue, catch a fly and flip the fly into its mouth in one second.

Frogs and toads shut their eyes when they swallow food. Their eyes sink down inside their heads and then pop out again. The large eyeballs help push down the food.

common toad

Food! Food! Food!

Frogs and toads eat insects and worms and slugs. But big frogs and toads eat bigger things. The African bullfrog eats lizards and mice. Sometimes it will even eat a whole chicken.

African
bullfrog

Did you know...
When a frog or a toad catches something horrible – a spiky stag beetle or a bug that tastes nasty – it spits it out.

▶ Eggs and tadpoles

Frogs and toads lay their eggs in water. The eggs are wrapped in jelly, to keep them warm.

Most frogs and toads lay lots of eggs.

The eggs are called spawn. Frogspawn is laid in a mass. Toadspawn is laid in strings.

frogspawn

toadspawn

After a while, the spawn hatches.
The young are called tadpoles.
They are tiny, no more than a
head and a tail.

tadpoles hatching
from frogspawn

Mostly, tadpoles eat pond
slime and water plants.

They grow bigger.

They grow back legs.

Then they grow front legs.

Their tails get smaller.

tadpole
in danger

▶ Danger!

The eggs and
the tadpoles are
always in danger.
They may be
eaten by fishes.
Or newts. Or ducks.
Or even other frogs. Sometimes,
tadpoles eat each other.

The young frogs and toads climb out
of the water.

Their stumpy tails will soon vanish.
They eat slugs and snails, worms and
insects. They grow until their skins
split – but it's all right, there's
a new skin underneath.

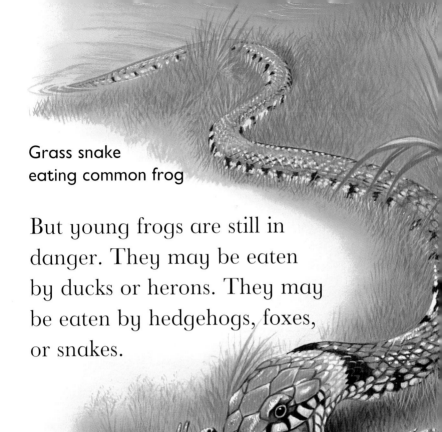

Grass snake
eating common frog

But young frogs are still in
danger. They may be eaten
by ducks or herons. They may
be eaten by hedgehogs, foxes,
or snakes.

Some are eaten by humans,
and some are run over by cars
or lawnmowers.

But most of them escape. How?

23

They may leap out
of danger.

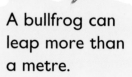

A bullfrog can
leap more than
a metre.

A common frog can
leap a long way.

They may swim out of danger.
They may hide from danger.
It's very hard to see this
Asian leaf frog.

Asian leaf frog

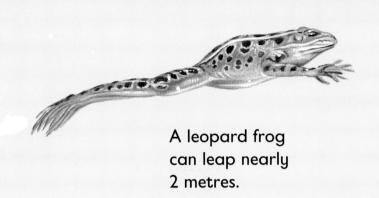

A leopard frog
can leap nearly
2 metres.

This toad has a different plan.
It puffs itself up to twice its size
in order to frighten off a snake.

common
toad

poison arrow frogs

Some frogs and toads are poisonous.

The poison is on their skins.
Poisonous frogs are brightly
coloured. The bright colours
warn hungry animals to beware.

26

Water matters

All frogs need water but no frogs drink. They take in water through their skins. All frogs need water but they can live in very dry places. They can even live in deserts.

The water-holding frog of Australia lives in the desert. It wraps itself in slime and burrows underground. The slime becomes firm, like packaging. This holds water in, and keeps the frog damp.

The water-holding frog may lie like this for two long years.

When the rainy season comes,
the frog wakes. It breaks out of
its slime-package.

The rainy season is very short, so
it must live its life at great speed.
Quickly it eats the insects that have
hatched in the rain ... quickly it
finds a mate ... quickly it lays its
eggs ... the eggs hatch in just one
day ... the tadpoles grow so fast
you could see it happening.

By the time the rains are over,
they are young froglets.

Now the water-holding frogs take
in water through their skins. Soon
they are nearly as round as balls.
Now they are ready to hide from
the dry days and nights.

At this moment, in a desert in Australia,
a frog sleeps. It is deep in a burrow.
It is curled up with its eyes closed.
It is waiting for the rains to fall.

Glossary

 amphibian An amphibian is an animal that lives on land and in water.   **7, 8**

 bulge To bulge means to swell outwards.   **16**

 burrow A burrow is a hole or tunnel dug by a small animal.   **4, 29**

 desert A desert is a dry place with little water where very few plants can grow.   **4, 27, 29**

 glide To glide means to float on the air.   **5**

 hatch To hatch means to break out of an egg, like a chicken or a tadpole.   **20, 28**

marsh A marsh is a wet and watery place where lots of marsh plants grow. **8**

 marsupial A marsupial is an animal which carries its babies in a pouch, like a kangaroo. **6**

 poisonous A poisonous thing has poison in it or on it. Strong poison can kill you. **26**

OXFORD

WILD READS

WILD READS will help your child develop a love of reading and a lasting curiosity about our world. See the websites and places to visit below to learn more about frogs and toads.

Frogs and Toads

WEBSITES

http://www.bbc.co.uk/cbbc/wild/amazinganimals/

http://kids.nationalgeographic.com/

http://www.froglife.org/

PLACES TO VISIT

Chester Zoo

http://www.chesterzoo.org/

Find a wetland centre near you
http://www.wwt.org.uk/

The best time to see frogs and toads is in spring. Take a trip to your local park and pond, to see them in their natural habitat.